W9-ANC-877

HAYNER PUBLIC LIBRARY DISTRICT
ALTON, ILLINOIS

OVERDUES .10 PER DAY MAXIMUM FINE
COST OF BOOKS. LOST OR DAMAGED
BOOKS ADDITIONAL $5.00 SERVICE CHARGE.

Investigating Science

What does a magnet do?

Jacqui Bailey

A⁺

Smart Apple Media

HAYNER PUBLIC LIBRARY DISTRICT
ALTON, ILLINOIS

First published in 2005 by Franklin Watts
96 Leonard Street, London EC2A 4XD

Franklin Watts Australia
45-51 Huntley Street, Alexandria, NSW 2015

This edition published under license from Franklin Watts. All rights reserved. Copyright © 2005 Franklin Watts

Editor: Jennifer Schofield, **Design:** Rachel Hamdi/Holly Mann, **Picture researcher:** Diana Morris, **Photography:** Andy Crawford, unless otherwise acknowledged

Acknowledgements:
Gerard Dryer/Africa Imagery/Afripics/Photographers Direct: 18t. Vanya Edwards/Sovfoto/Eastfoto/Photographers Direct: 29b. Simon Fraser/SPL: 20t. Ray Moller: 3.NASA: 28. Eric Needham/Ecoscene: 22. Tony Page/Ecoscene: 29c. Sinclair Stammers/SPL: 7b. Watts: 27b.

With thanks to our models: Chandler Durbridge, Charlie Spicer, Ashleigh Munns, Emel Augustine, Keyon Duffus

Published in the United States by Smart Apple Media
2140 Howard Drive West, North Mankato, Minnesota 56003

U.S. publication copyright © 2007 Smart Apple Media
International copyright reserved in all countries. No part of this book may be reproduced in any form without written permission from the publisher.
Printed in the United States of America

Library of Congress Cataloging-in-Publication Data

Bailey, Jacqui.
What does a magnet do? / by Jacqui Bailey.
p. cm. — (Investigating science)
ISBN-13 : 978-1-58340-929-9
Includes index.
1. Magnets—Juvenile literature. I. Title.

QC757.5.B35 2006
538'.4—dc22   2005052330

9 8 7 6 5 4 3 2 1

Contents

j538.4
BAI

b17428725

What are magnets?   6

Magnetic materials   8

Pulling power   10

Poles apart   12

An invisible force   14

Strength of force   16

Magnetic magic   18

Moving with magnets   20

Sorting with magnets   22

Floating with magnets   24

Pointing the way   26

Useful words   28

Index   30

What are magnets?

Magnets are pieces of metal or stone that can make things stick to them.

THINK about the kinds of magnets you have seen.
- Some toys have magnets in them.
- Magnets come in all shapes and sizes.

Have you ever played with a magnet?

doughnut magnets

bar magnets

disc magnet

horseshoe magnet

You will need:

Scissors ✔

Some string ✔

A long pencil ✔

A doughnut magnet ✔

Some colored tagboard ✔

A permanent marker ✔

Some metal paper clips ✔

What do magnets do?

(1) Cut a length of string longer than your pencil. Tie one end to the pencil and the other end to the magnet. This is your "fishing rod."

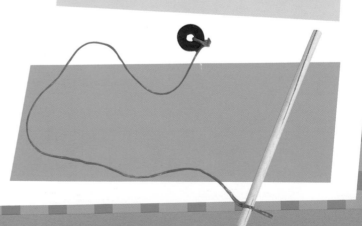

2 Cut some fish shapes out of the tagboard. Number each fish. Then, attach a paper clip to each fish.

3 Put the fish on the ground or in a large bowl.

4 Lower the magnet over the fish. Can you catch any fish? If you play with a friend, you can take turns fishing. When all of the fish have been caught, add up the numbers of your "catch" and see who has the highest score.

Because . . .

The magnet pulls the fish off of the ground because the paper clip on the fish sticks to the magnet. This is because the magnet is pulling the metal paper clip toward it. Most magnets are made of the metals iron or **steel***. There is also a magnetic rock called* **lodestone** *(left), or magnetite.*

Magnetic materials

Some objects stick to magnets, and others do not.

THINK about where you would find magnets in your home.
- Refrigerator doors have small magnets to keep the door shut.
- Magnets can decorate the refrigerator door.

What kind of objects stick to magnets?

You will need:

A pencil and a ruler ✔

A sheet of paper ✔

A strong magnet, such as a bar magnet ✔

Some test objects (e.g. a coin, an eraser, a key, a wooden spoon, a metal spoon, a plastic cup, some thumbtacks, some scraps of paper) ✔

Which materials are magnetic?

(1) Use the pencil and ruler to divide your paper into three columns. Name the first column "object," the second column "guess," and the third column "result."

2 List your test objects in the first column.

3 In the second column, put a check mark next to the objects you think will stick to the magnet, and an "X" next to those you think will not.

4 Test each object and put a check mark or an "X" in the third column. How many of your guesses were correct?

Because . . .

*Objects stick to magnets because they have iron in them. Materials that have iron in them are called **magnetic materials**. Materials with no iron in them, such as tin, brass, paper, and wood, are non-magnetic. These materials do not stick to magnets.*

Do not test your magnets on music or video tapes and discs. Do not use magnets near televisions and computers—the magnets could damage them.

Pulling power

A **force** is a pull or push. The pulling power of magnets is a force called **magnetism**.

THINK about different kinds of force.

● You lift a glass using the force of your muscles.

● A magnet pulls on a paper clip using magnetism.

Can you see magnetism work?

You will need:

A pen and a ruler ✔

A piece of paper ✔

A strong bar magnet ✔

Some paper clips ✔

A horseshoe magnet ✔

How does magnetism work?

① Use the ruler to draw a straight line along the long edge of the paper. Mark each half inch (1.2 cm) for five inches (12.2 cm) from the top of the piece of paper.

2 Draw a line across the page at the five-inch (12.2 cm) and half-inch (1.2 cm) marks. These are your start and finish lines.

3 Place the bar magnet on the start line and the paper clip on the finish line.

4 Slowly slide the bar magnet along the paper toward the paper clip. How far away is the magnet from the paper clip before anything happens?

5 Try the test again using the horseshoe magnet instead of the bar magnet. What happens?

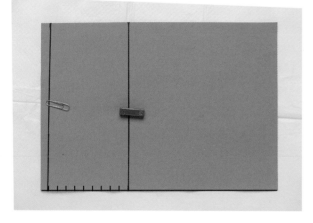

Because . . .

The paper clip moves toward the magnet because it is **attracted***, or pulled, to the magnet by the force of magnetism. Magnets have different strengths. How far away the magnet is before it attracts the paper clip depends on the strength of your magnet.*

Poles apart

Magnetism is stronger at the ends of a magnet than in the middle.

THINK about a bar magnet.

- The ends of a magnet are known as its **poles**.
- Sometimes the poles are different colors. They may also be marked with the letters "N" and "S," for north and south pole.

How are the poles of a magnet different?

north pole   south pole

You will need:

Some tape ✔

2 toy cars ✔

2 bar magnets at least as long as the cars ✔

What happens when different poles touch?

1. Tape the middle of each magnet to the roof of a toy car. Make sure both magnets have the same pole pointing to the front of the car.

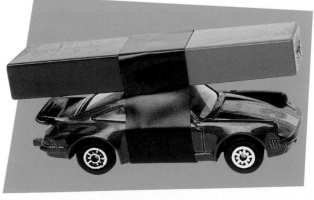

12

2 What happens when you push the front of one car toward the back of the other?

3 What happens when you push both cars face to face?

4 What happens if you put the cars back to back?

Because . . .

When one car is behind the other, the magnets pull the cars together. This is because the opposite poles are facing each other (north to south, or south to north). Opposite magnetic poles attract each other.

When the two cars are facing each other or when they are back to back, the magnets push the cars apart. This is because the same poles are facing each other (north to north or south to south). The same magnetic poles **repel**, or push away from, each other.

An invisible force

Magnetism is an invisible force—you cannot see it. It can pull on things without touching them.

THINK about how magnetism works.
- The paper clip on pages 10–11 jumped toward the magnet before the magnet touched it.
- Magnetism can reach through the air to pull on something.

How far does magnetism reach?

You will need:
Plastic wrap ✔
A bar magnet ✔
A disc magnet ✔
A jar of iron filings (or steel wool chopped into small pieces) ✔
A piece of paper ✔

How does magnetism surround a magnet?

(1) Wrap both magnets in plastic wrap. Place the paper on top of the bar magnet, so that the magnet is in the middle.

(2) Sprinkle the iron filings (or steel wool) onto the paper, circling the spot where the magnet is. What happens?

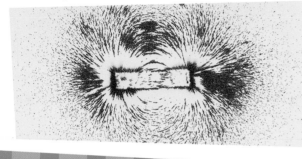

(3) Lift the paper and carefully pour your filings back into the jar.

(4) Replace the bar magnet with the disc magnet. Shake the filings onto the paper again. What happens this time?

Because . . .

The iron filings form lines on the paper. These lines show how the magnetic force (magnetism) pulls the iron filings toward the magnet. Different-shaped magnets make different patterns. The filings are usually thickest at the poles, but other lines spread out from the magnet, or curve from pole to pole. These lines show how far from the magnet its magnetic force reaches. This area is called its **magnetic field**.

Strength of force

A magnetic field can reach through non-magnetic materials.

THINK about what refrigerator magnets do.

• A refrigerator magnet will hold a piece of paper on a magnetic surface such as a metal door.

• But paper is non-magnetic and will not stick to the magnet on its own.

How strong is a magnetic field?

You will need:
Scissors ✔
Paper ✔
A bar magnet ✔
Tape ✔
A paper clip ✔

How strong is a magnetic field?

① Cut the paper into several squares. Make the squares large enough to wrap around the magnet.

2 Check that the magnet will pick up the paper clip.

3 Wrap the magnet in one layer of paper and pick up the paper clip.

4 Repeat step three a number of times, adding an extra layer of paper each time.

5 How do the different layers of paper affect the magnet?

Because . . .

The magnet should pick up the paper clip through at least one layer of paper. This is because its magnetic force spreads outward, as we saw on pages 14–15. But if the magnet is wrapped in layer upon layer of paper, the layers will gradually block the magnetic force, and the magnet will no longer work.

Magnetic magic

Magnetism can work through most materials, including water.

THINK about what water is.
- Everything in the world is made of some kind of material.
- Water is a liquid material. It flows in streams, lakes, seas, and oceans.

Can you use a magnet to pull something out of water?

You will need:

A glass jar ✔
Water ✔
A paper clip ✔
A magnet ✔
Some string ✔

Do magnets work through water?

① Almost fill the glass jar with water.

2 Drop in the paper clip and let it sink to the bottom of the jar.

3 What happens if you hold the magnet to the outside of the jar near the paper clip? Can you make the paper clip move? Can you lift it to the top of the jar?

4 Repeat step two, but this time, tie a piece of string around the magnet and lower it into the water. Will it pick up the paper clip?

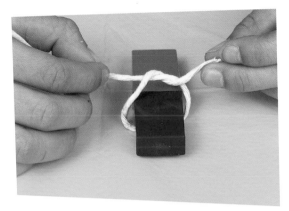

Because . . .

You can use the magnet to slide the paper clip up the side of the glass jar because its magnetic field passes through the glass and the water to pull on the paper clip. If you put the magnet into the water, it will still work on the paper clip because water is non-magnetic and does not block the magnetic field.

Moving with magnets

The pulling power of magnets can be used in different ways.

You will need:

A permanent marker ✔

A large piece of stiff cardboard ✔

2 pieces of tagboard about 2 inches (5 cm) square ✔

4 soup cans ✔

2 paper clips ✔

2 disc magnets ✔

2 rulers ✔

Tape ✔

Scissors ✔

A watch ✔

THINK about how magnets are used to move things.

● A crane with a large magnet hanging from it is used to lift and move heavy blocks of metal in a scrapyard.

How can you use magnets?

Can you make a magnetic game?

① Use the permanent marker to draw a squiggly road on the large piece of cardboard.

2 Make a fold across the middle of each piece of tagboard. Draw the shape of a car on the tagboard above the fold. Cut the fold into two flaps and fold them in opposite directions so that the cars are able to stand upright.

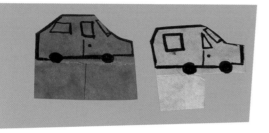

3 Prop up the large piece of cardboard with cans at each corner so that there is a clear gap beneath it. Then, slide a paper clip onto the front flap of each car and place the cars at the beginning of the road.

4 Tape a magnet to the end of each ruler and slide the magnets underneath the cardboard to move the cars. How long does it take each player to move his or her car to the end of the road?

Because . . .

The magnets can move the cars around the road because their magnetic force passes through the cardboard and attracts the metal paper clips attached to the cars.

Sorting with magnets

Magnets can be used to separate some materials from others.

THINK about how magnets are used to separate things.

- Magnets separate iron and steel from other materials in a scrapyard.
  - Iron and steel are often recycled (used again). Magnets separate steel cans from aluminum cans so they can be recycled.

Why not make your own can sorter?

You will need:

Some string ✔

A strong magnet ✔

Some clean, empty soup and pop cans ✔

What kind of metal is it?

1 Tie a piece of string as long as your leg to the magnet.

2 Stand the cans in a line on the floor.

3 Hold the string in your hand, and slowly move the magnet over the line of cans. What happens? Which cans are attracted to the magnet, and which ones are not?

Because . . .

Some of the cans will be attracted to the magnet, but others will not. This is because some cans are made of steel, which is a magnetic material, and some are made of aluminum, which is a non-magnetic material. Which types of food and drink are stored in steel cans, and which types are stored in aluminum cans?

Floating with magnets

The pushing force of magnets is also useful.

THINK about how magnets repel (push away from) each other.

• The cars on pages 12–13 repelled each other when they were back-to-back.

Can you use this pushing force to make a magnet float?

You will need:

3 doughnut magnets ✔

Colored paper ✔

Scissors ✔

A glue stick or tape ✔

A wooden rod almost as thick as the hole in the magnets ✔

Clay ✔

How can you make magnets float?

1 Find out which side of your magnets stick together. As opposite poles attract, one side will be a north pole, and the other will be a south pole.

2 Cut out a small square of colored paper. Glue or tape the square onto the north side of each magnet.

3 Push the wooden rod into a lump of clay so that it stands upright.

4 Slide the first magnet onto the wooden rod north side up, the second magnet north side down, and the third magnet north side up. What happens to the magnets?

Because . . .

The magnets float apart because they all have the same poles facing each other. North to north or south to south poles repel each other. Without the wooden rod, the magnets would slip sideways and drop to the table, but the rod holds them in place, keeping the poles facing each other.

Pointing the way

A **compass** helps people find their way from place to place. Magnets have been used in compasses for hundreds of years.

THINK about how compasses work.

• A compass has a needle that swings around as the compass is moved.

• The needle is a magnet. Its ends always point north and south.

How can you make a magnet work like a compass?

You will need:

A piece of paper ✔

Tape ✔

A piece of string ✔

A bar magnet ✔

A pen and a ruler ✔

A pocket compass (keep this away from the bar magnet) ✔

How does a compass work?

① Tape the sheet of paper onto a table top or the floor.

2 Tie one end of the string around the middle of the bar magnet so that it balances when you hold it up.

3 Hold the magnet just above the paper and keep your hand still. When the magnet stops moving, it will point in a particular direction.

4 Carefully lower the magnet onto the paper. Without moving the magnet, mark where the two poles of the magnet lie on the paper.

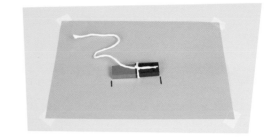

5 Remove the magnet and use a ruler to draw a line through the middle of the two marks. Place your compass on top of the line. How does your line compare with the compass needle?

Because . . .

The magnet line and the compass needle point in the same direction. This is because the bar magnet and the compass needle are lining up with Earth's magnetic poles. Earth itself is a giant magnet. Its magnetic poles are near the North Pole and South Pole.

Useful words

Attract is what a magnet does when it pulls something toward it. Attract is the opposite of repel.

Compass is an instrument that tells you which direction north and south are, no matter where you are on Earth. Some compasses work only in the northern hemisphere, and others work only in the southern hemisphere.

Force is a scientific word for a "push" or a "pull." A force makes an object move in a particular direction. It can also change a moving object's direction, slow it down, or speed it up. Magnetism is a force.

Lodestone is a type of rock that is naturally magnetic. More than 1,000 years ago, Chinese people used lodestones as compasses. Lodestone is also called magnetite.

Magnetic field is the area surrounding a magnet within which its magnetic force will work. When a magnetic material comes within reach of a magnetic field, it is pulled toward the magnet inside that field.

Magnetic Earth

Earth is surrounded by its own magnetic field. This is because the center of Earth is made of iron, and it acts like a giant magnet.

Magnetic materials are materials that are attracted to magnets. Any material that has iron in it is a magnetic material.

Magnetism is the pulling or pushing force that a magnet has.

Poles are the two ends of a magnet. Magnetism is strongest at the poles. On a disc magnet, the poles are the two flat faces.

Repel is what a magnet does when it pushes another magnet away from it.

Steel is a metal made from iron. Iron is found in the ground in rocks called ores.

Electrical magnets

A piece of metal can be made to work like a magnet by sending electricity through it. This type of magnet is called an electromagnet. Electromagnets work only while electricity is flowing through them. When the electricity is turned off, the magnet stops working.

Riding on air

A special type of train called a maglev train speeds along on a cushion of air instead of wheels. Strong magnets laid on the track repel other magnets under the train and lift the cars into the air.

Index

aluminum 22, 23
attraction 11, 13, 21, 23, 28, 29

bar magnets 6, 11, 12, 15, 27
brass 9

compass 26, 28
compass needle 26, 27
cranes 20

direction 28
disc magnets 6, 15, 29
doughnut magnets 6

Earth 27, 28
electricity
electromagnet 29

force 10, 11, 14, 15, 24, 28, 29

horseshoe magnets 6, 11

iron 7, 9, 22, 28, 29
iron filings 15

liquids 18
lodestone 7, 28

maglev trains 29

magnetic field 15, 16, 19, 28
magnetic force *see* magnetism
magnetic materials 9, 23, 28, 29
magnetic strength 11, 12, 16, 29
magnetism 10, 11, 12, 14, 15, 17, 18, 21, 28, 29
magnetite *see* lodestone
metals 6, 7, 16, 18, 20, 29

non-magnetic materials 9, 16, 19, 23

paper 9, 16
poles 12, 13, 15, 25, 27, 29
pulling 7, 10, 11, 13, 14, 15, 18, 20, 28, 29
pushing 10, 13, 24, 28, 29

recycling 22
refrigerator magnets 8, 16
repelling 13, 24, 25, 28, 29

scrapyards 20, 22
solids 18
steel 7, 22, 23

water 18, 19
wood 9